MY HEART

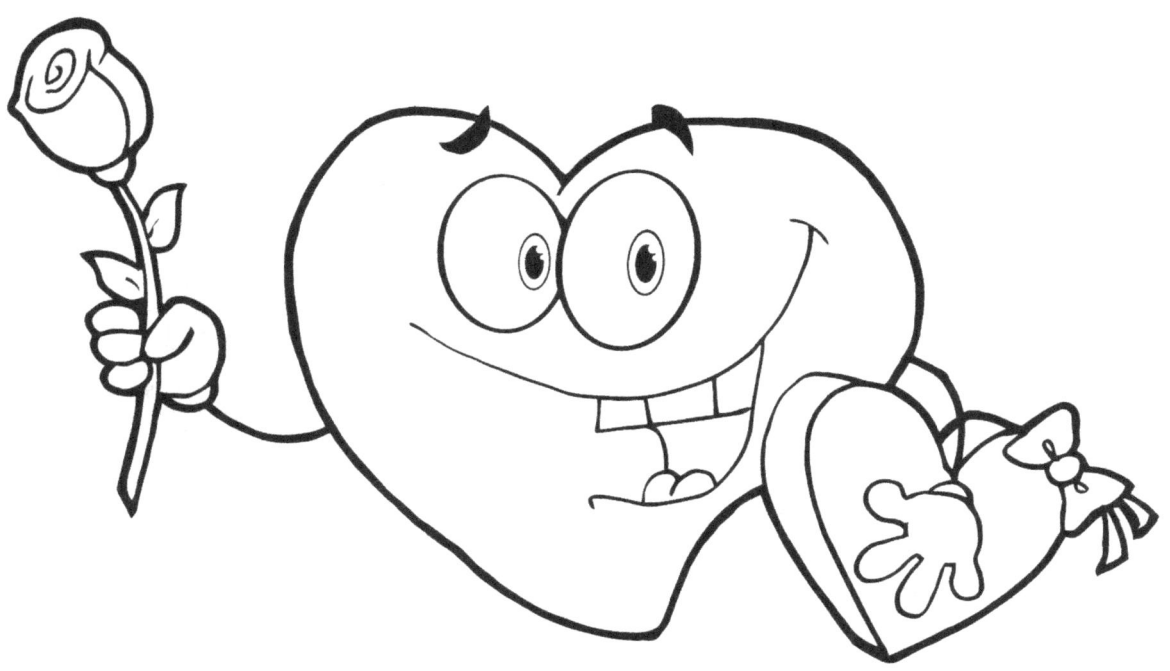

_____ WITH LOVE !

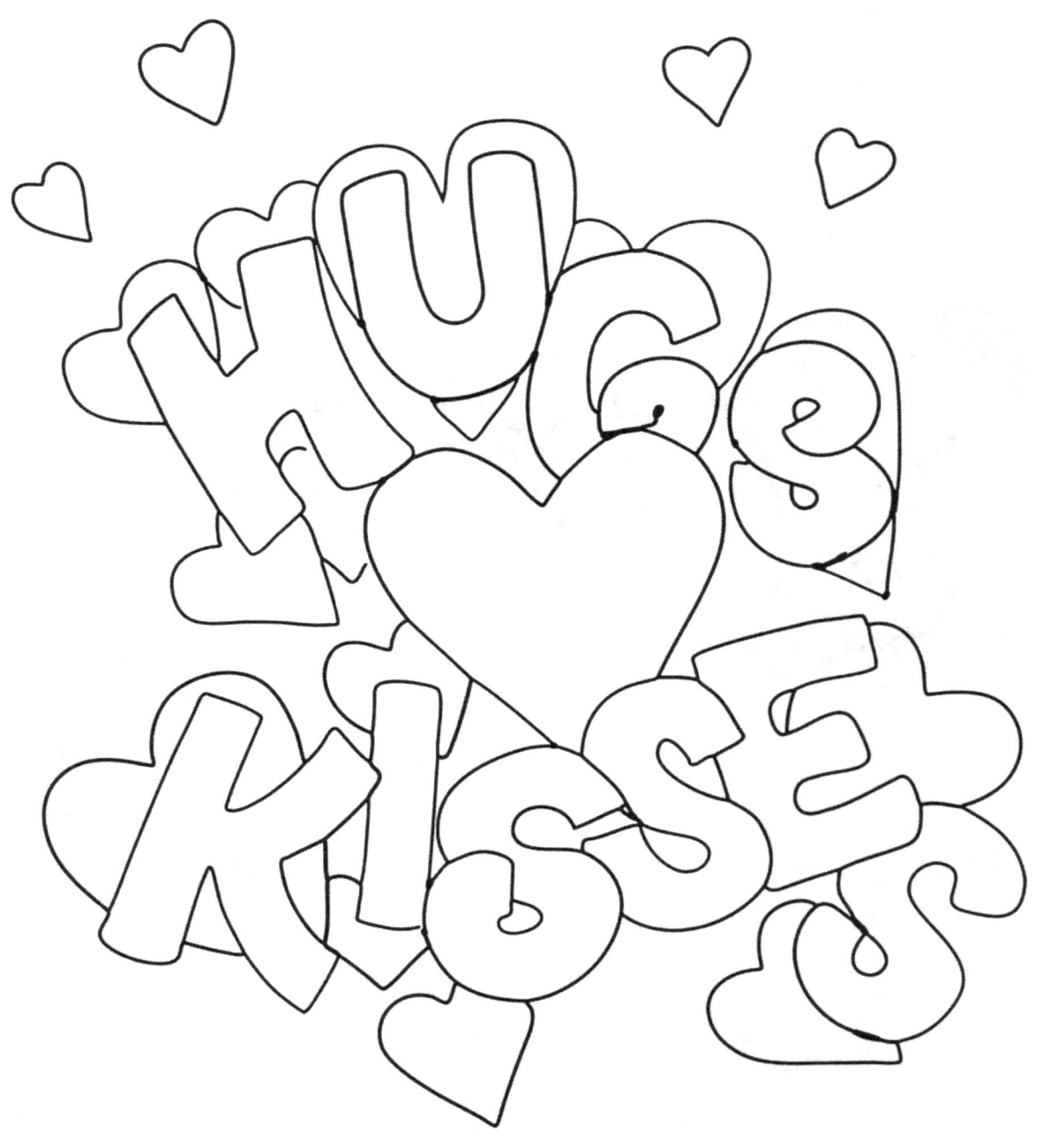

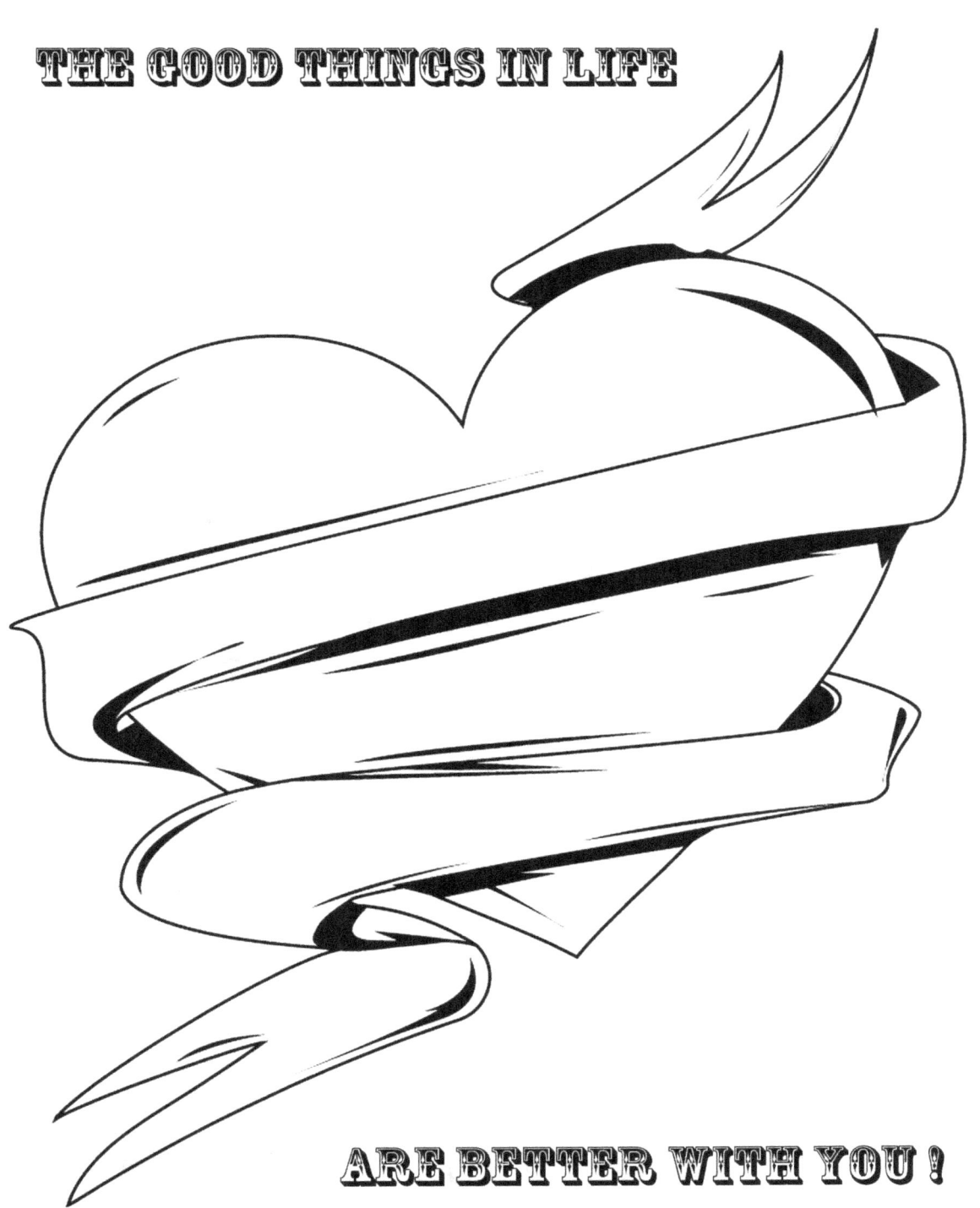

YOU KNOW YOU'RE IN LOVE WHEN YOU CAN'T FALL ASLEEP

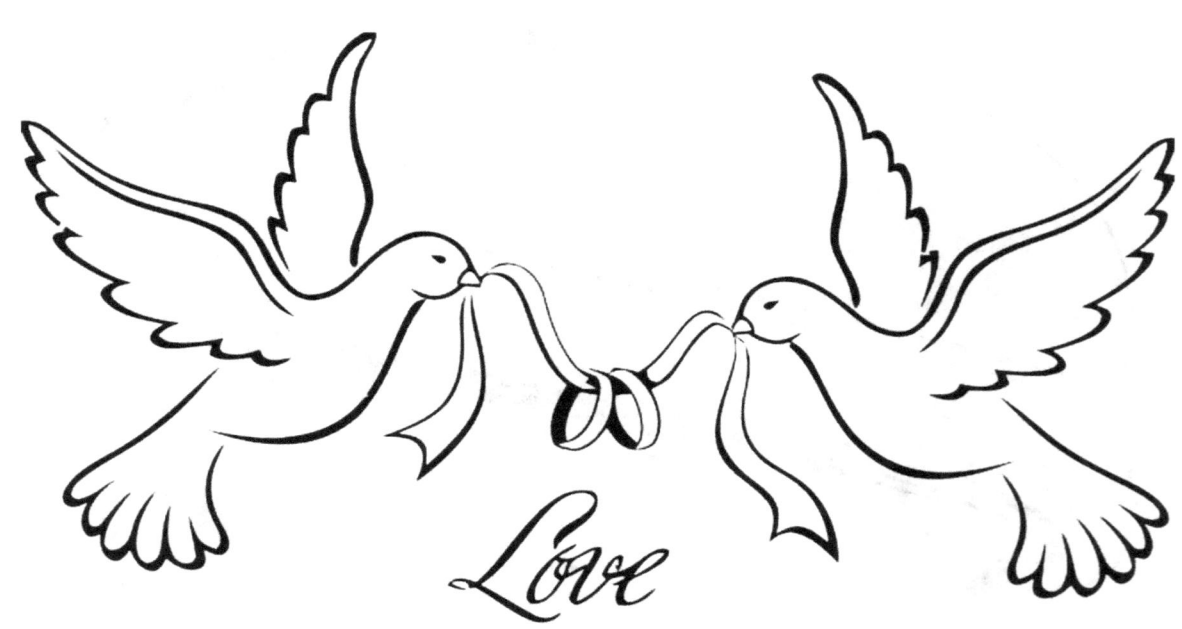

Love

BECAUSE REALITY IS FINALLY BETTER THAN YOUR DREAMS !

LIFE IST'T ALWAYS WONDERFIL,

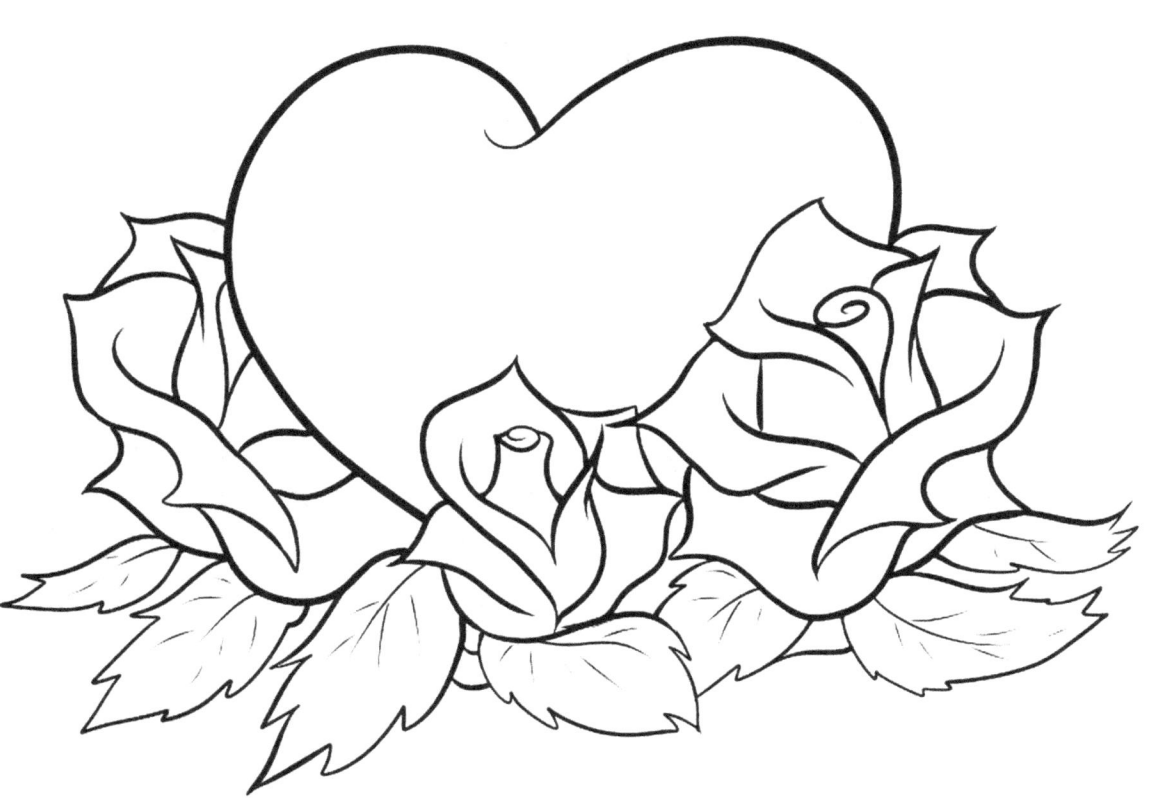

BUT YOU ARE !

LOVE IS OUR TRUE DESTINY.

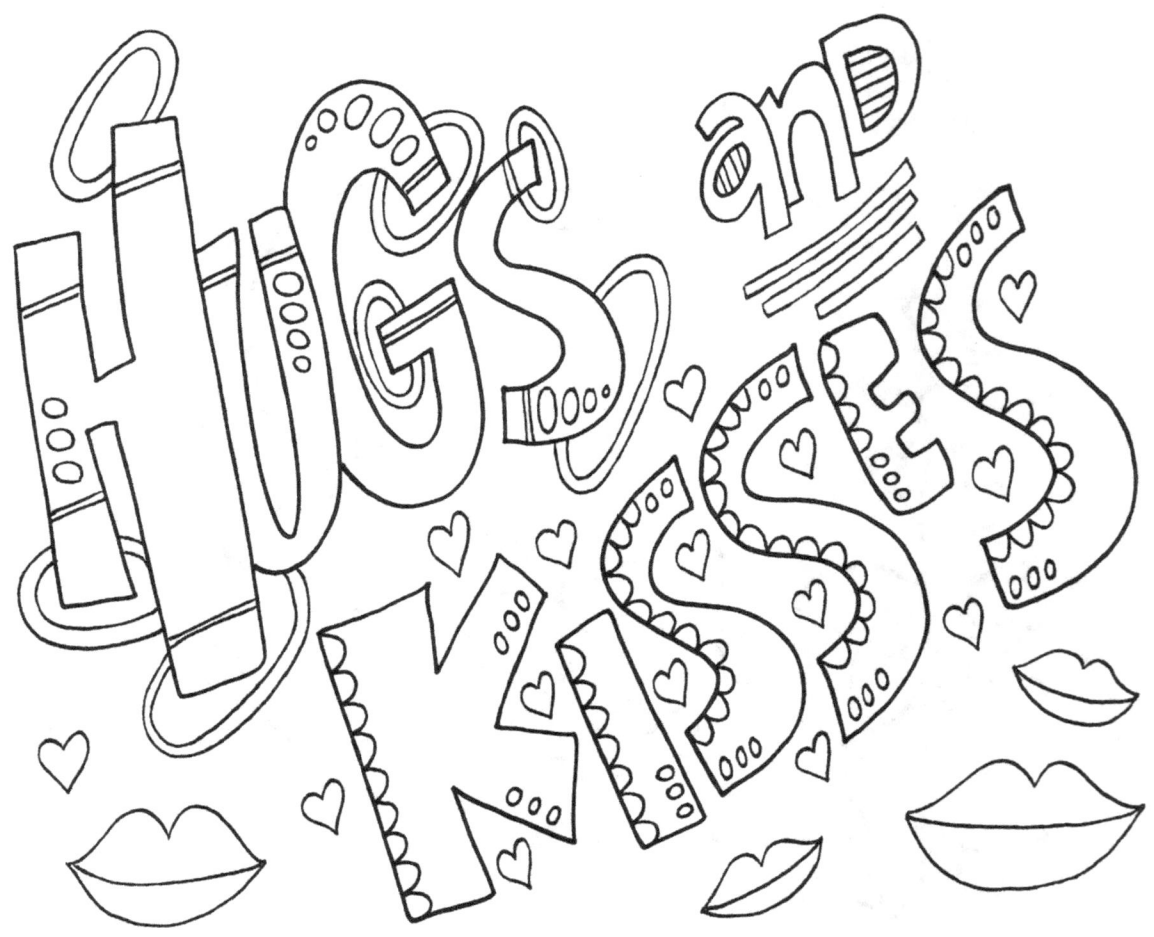

WE DO NOT FIND THE MEANING OF
LIFE BY OURSELVES ASONE
WE FIND IT WITH ANOTHER !

YOU ARE MY HEART'S EPIC ADVENTURE !

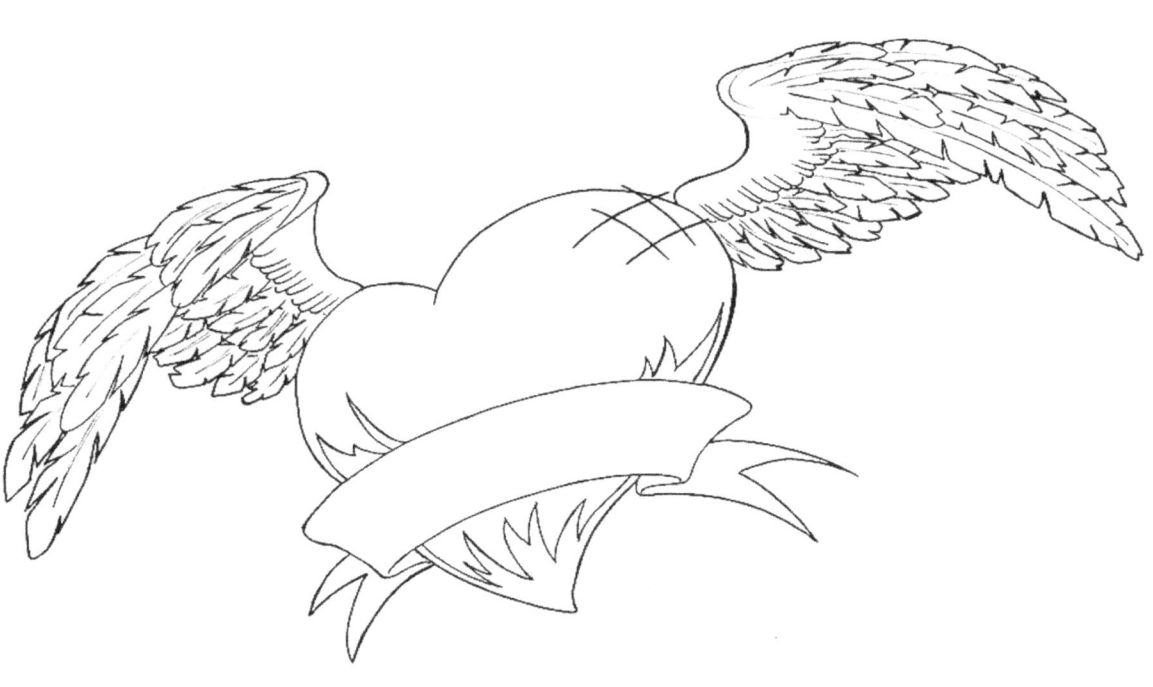

_____

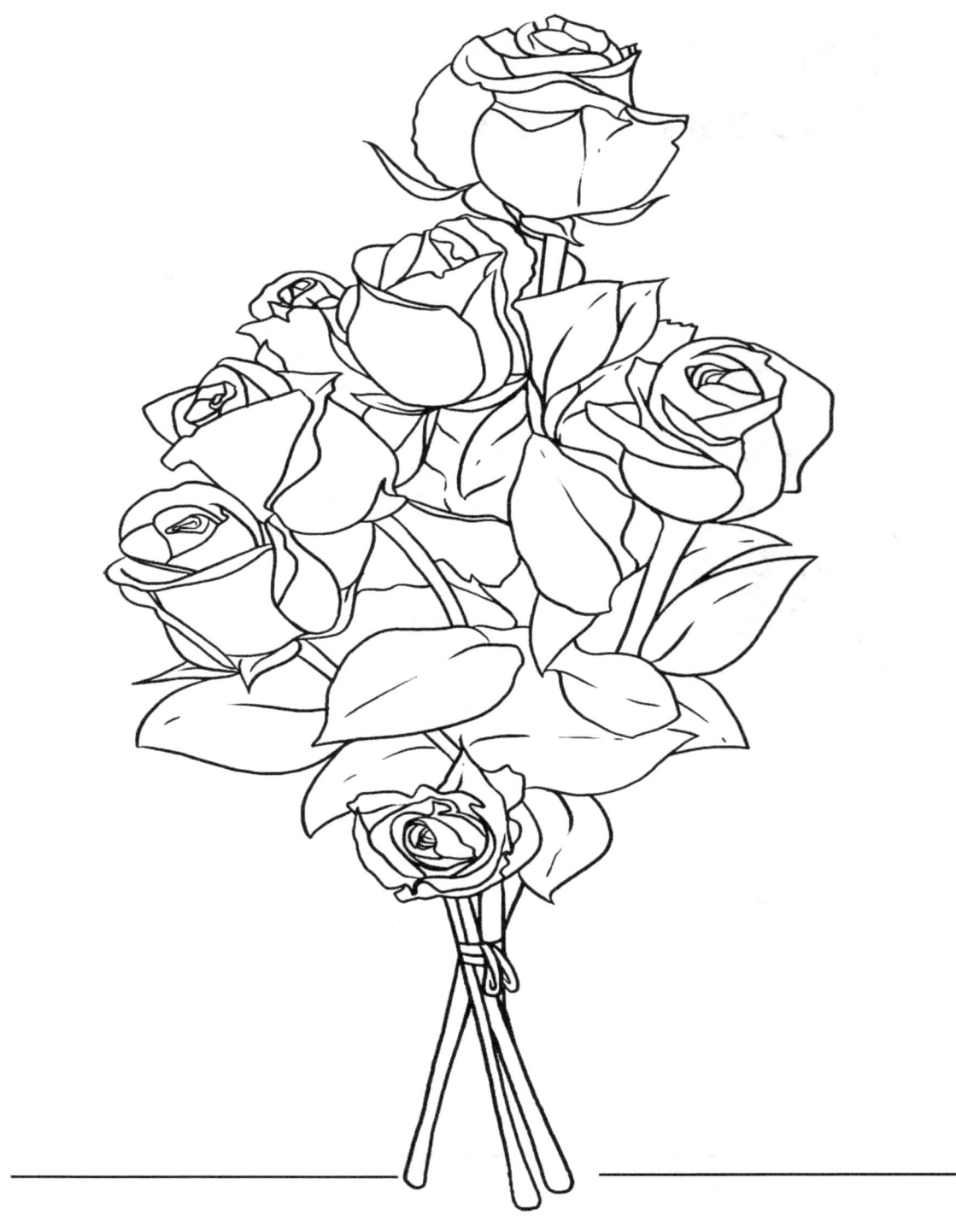

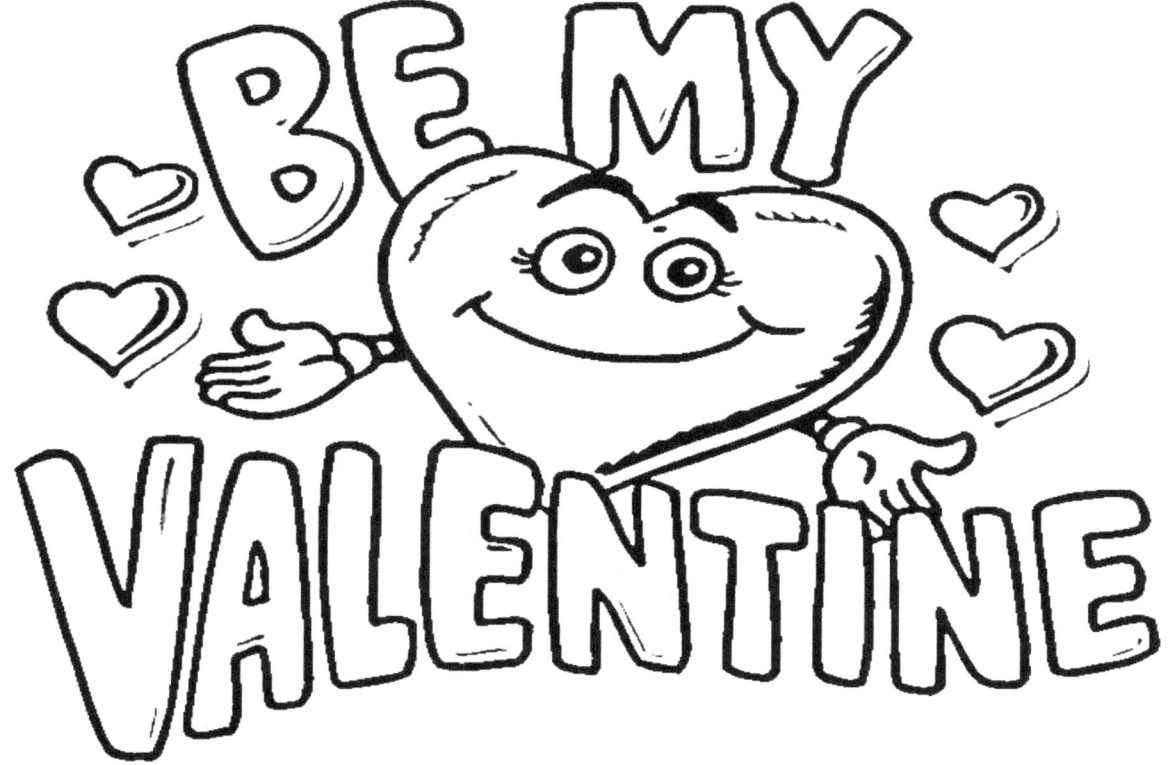

_____

_____

_____

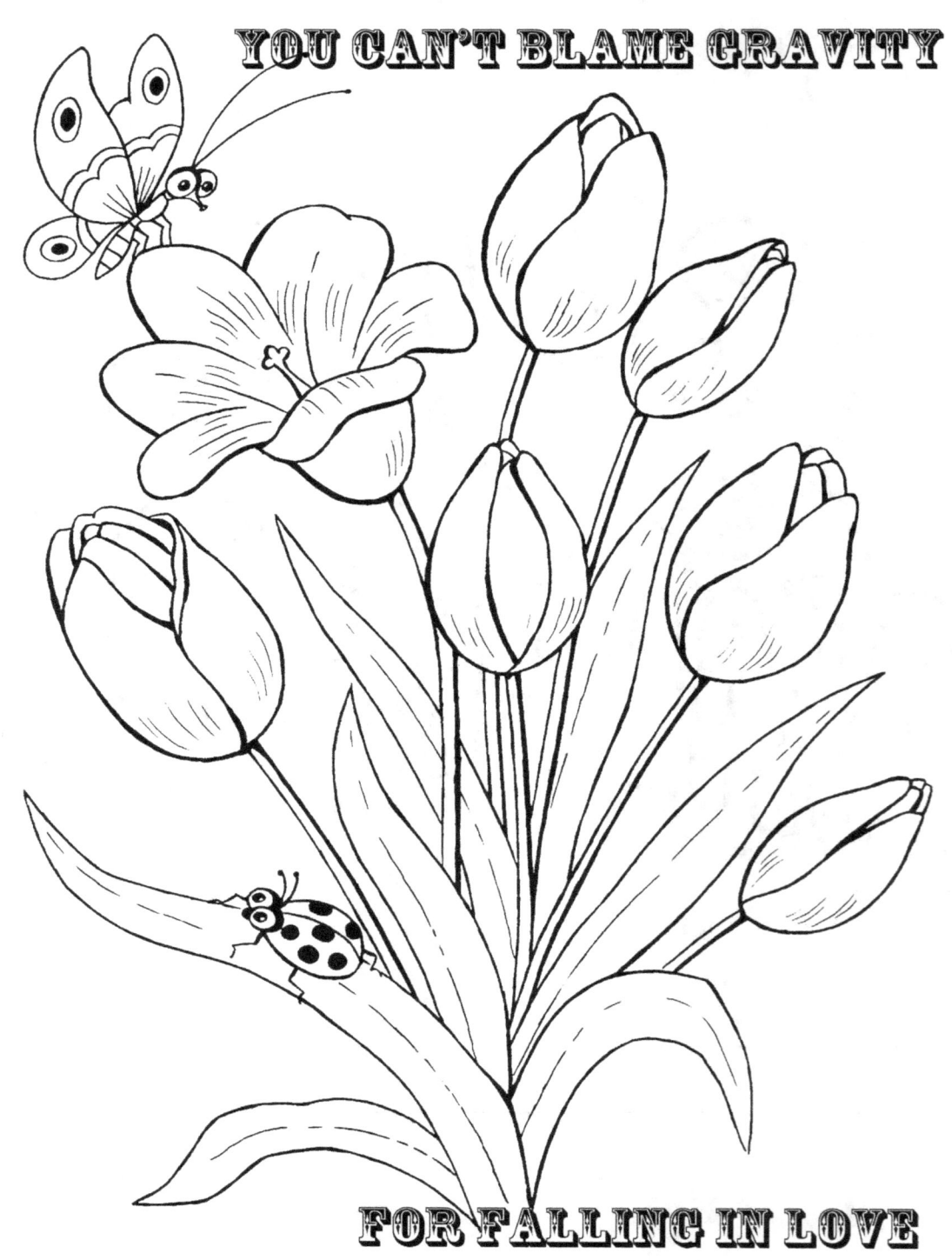

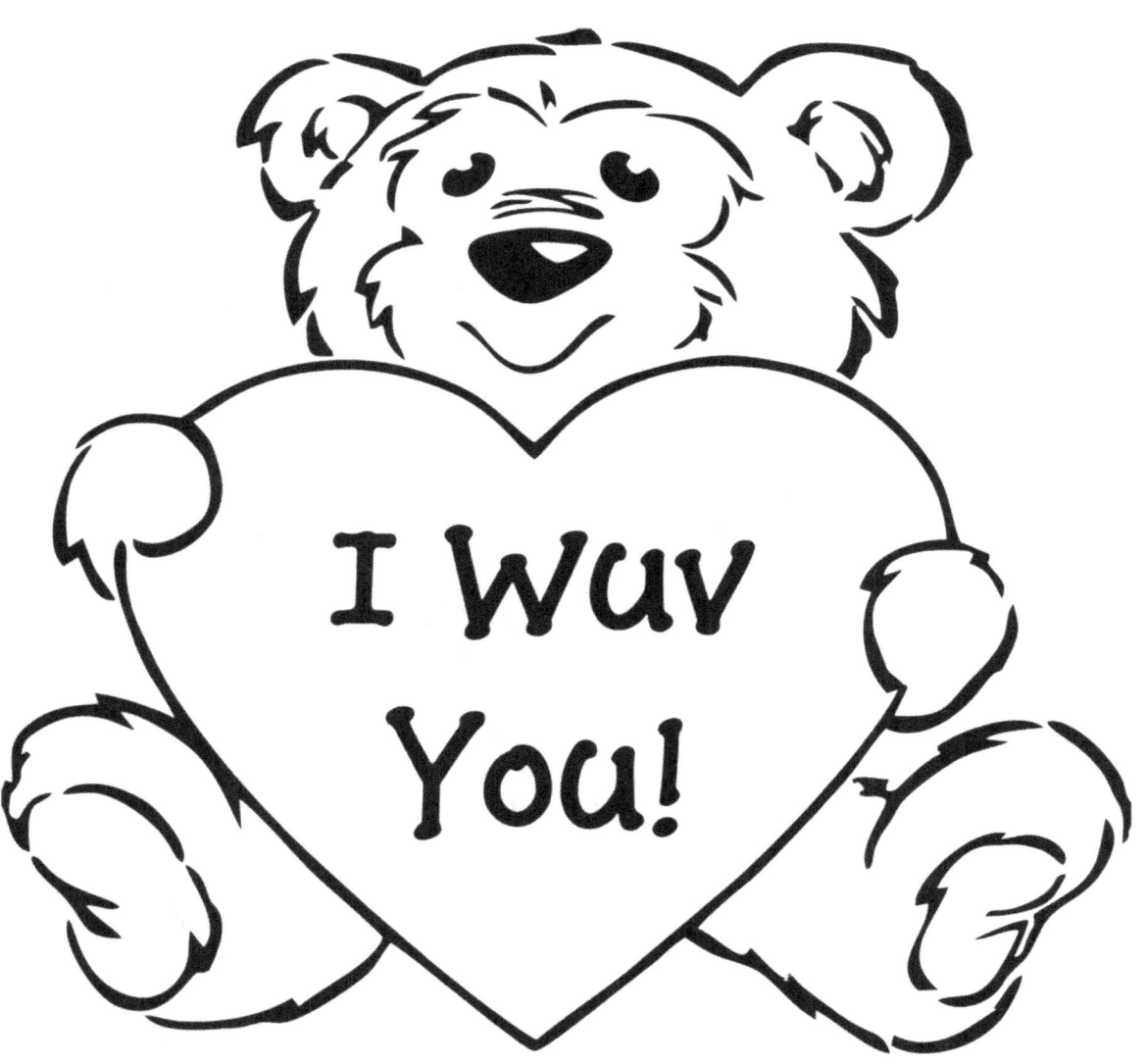

LOVE IS COMPOSED OF A SINGLE SOUL

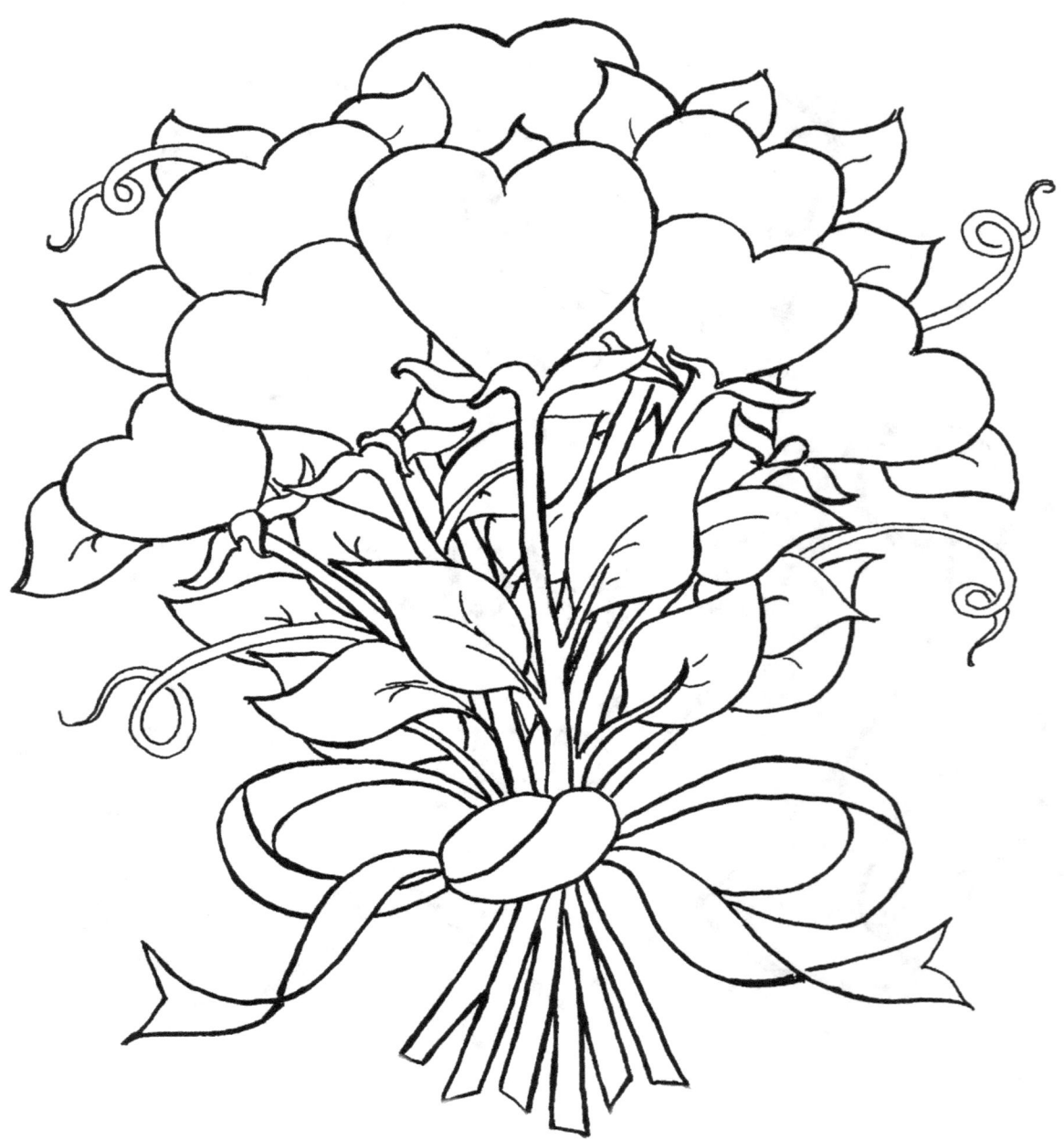

INHABITING TWO BODIES.

ALL YOU NEED IS LOVE

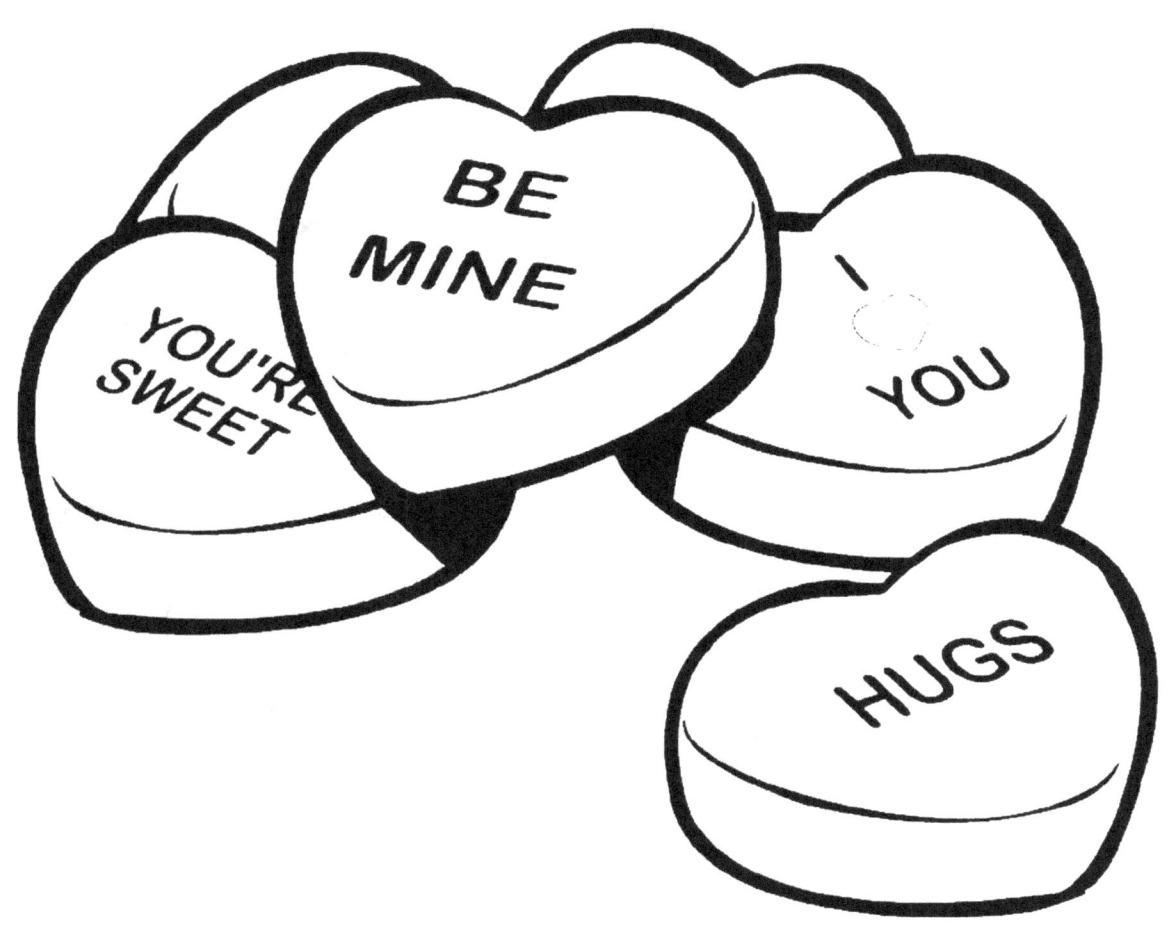

BUT A LITTLE CHOCOLATE NOW AND
THEN DOESN'T HURT !

TRUE LOVE STORIES

NEVER HAVE ENDINGS .

LOVE ISN'T SOMETHING YOU FIND.

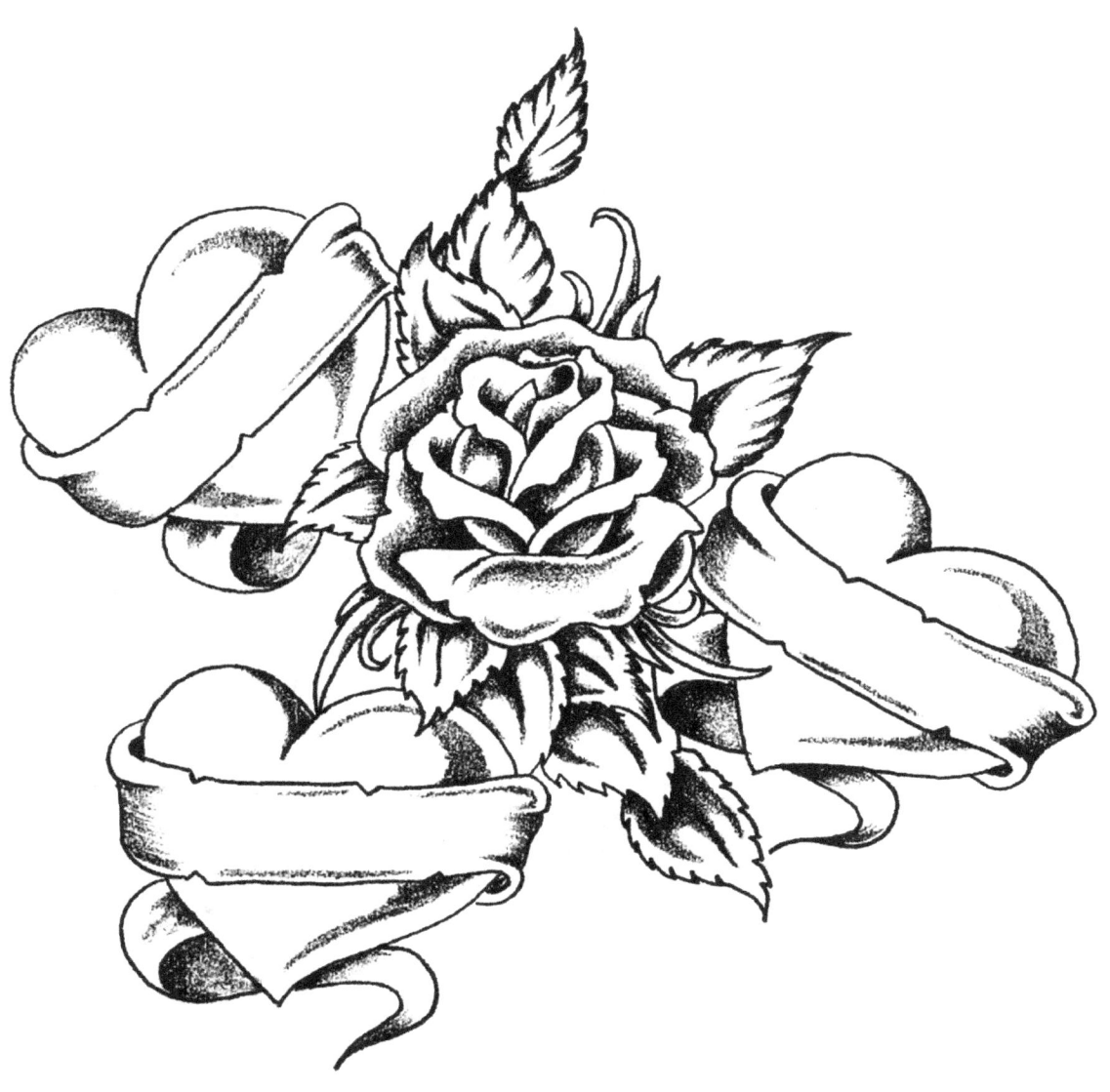

LOVE IS SOMETHING THAT FINDS YOU.

WHATEVER OUR SOULS MADE OF,

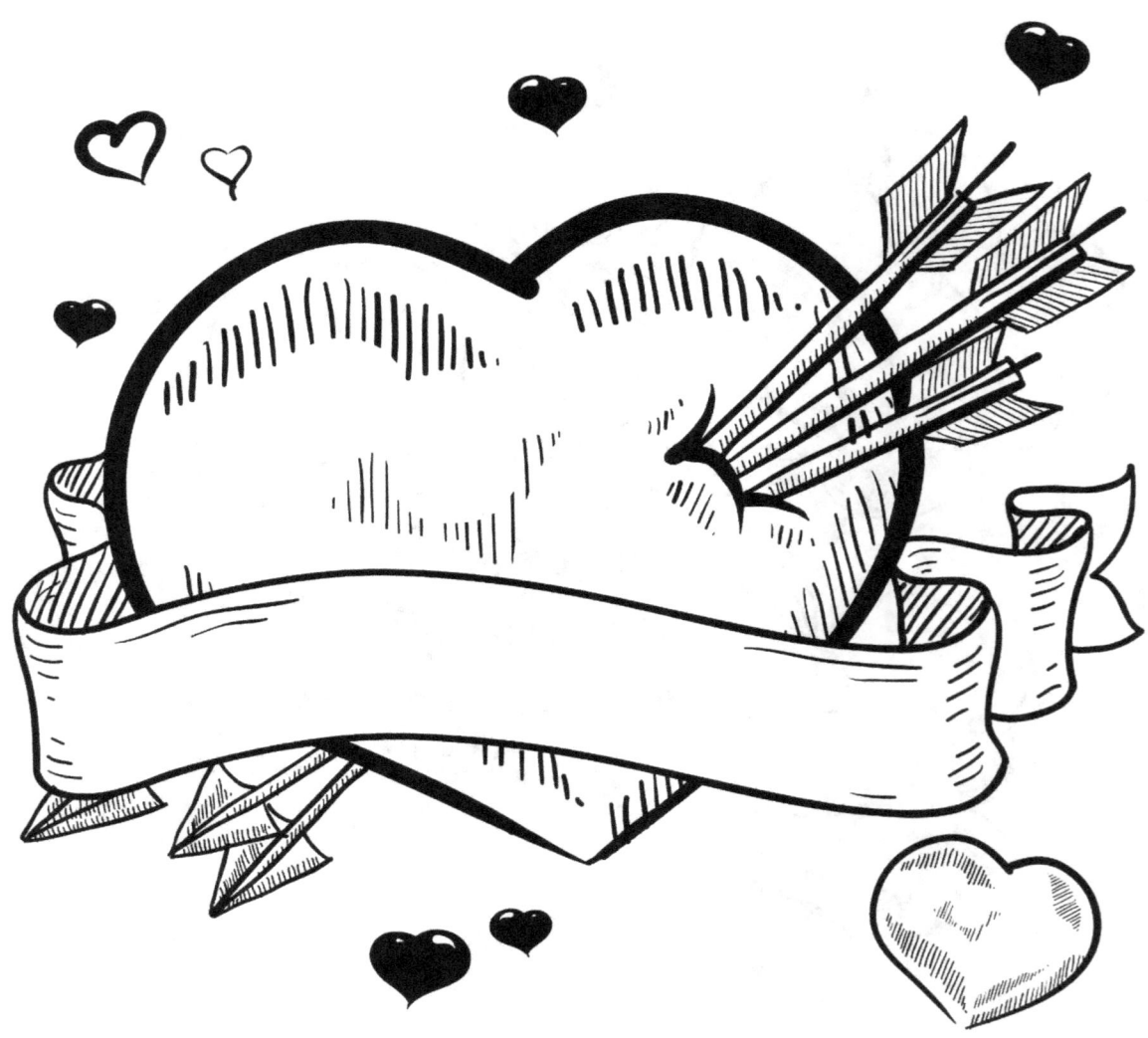

FOR LOVED ONES IT IS THE SAME.

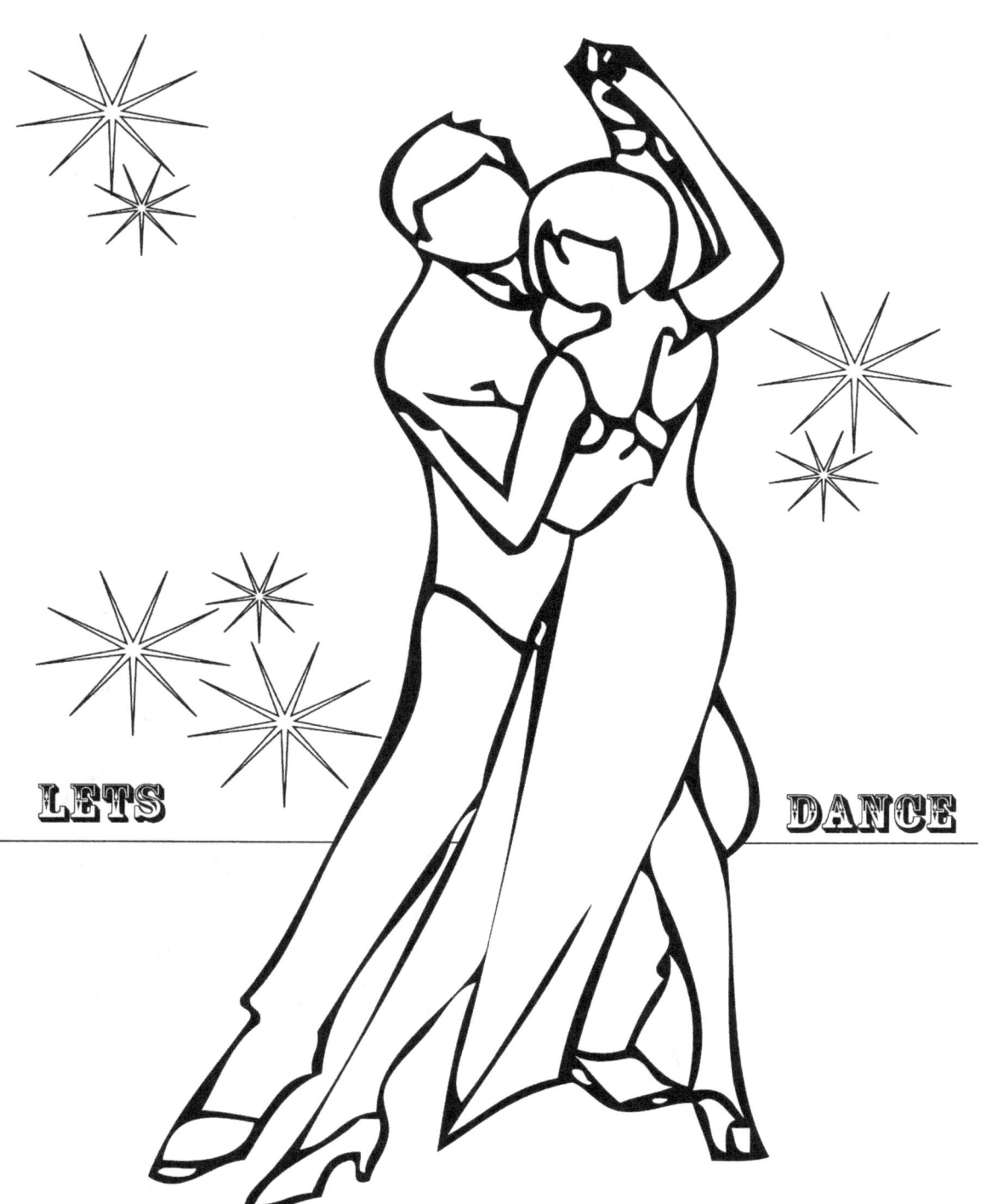

LETS DANCE

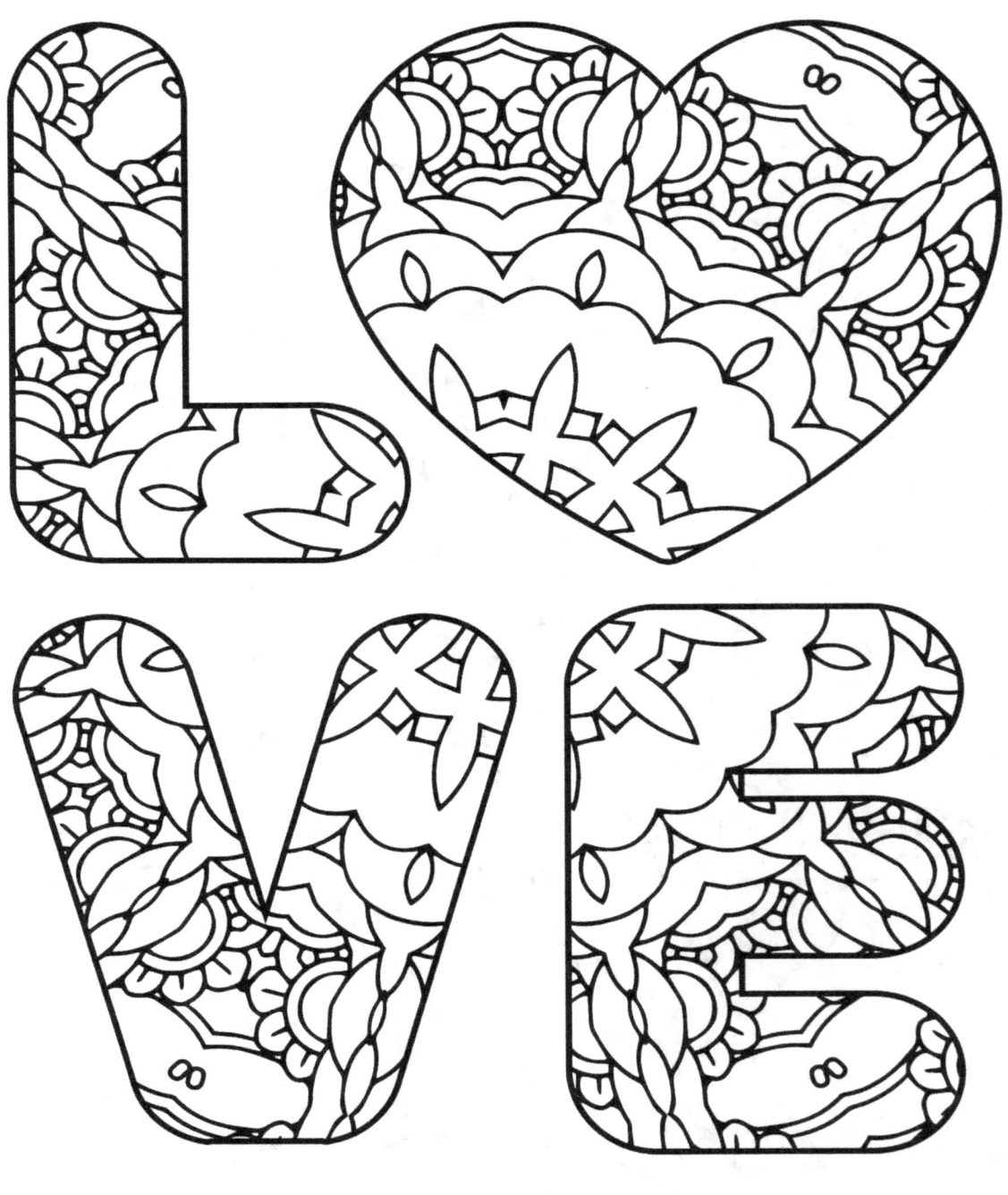

LOVE IS... _____

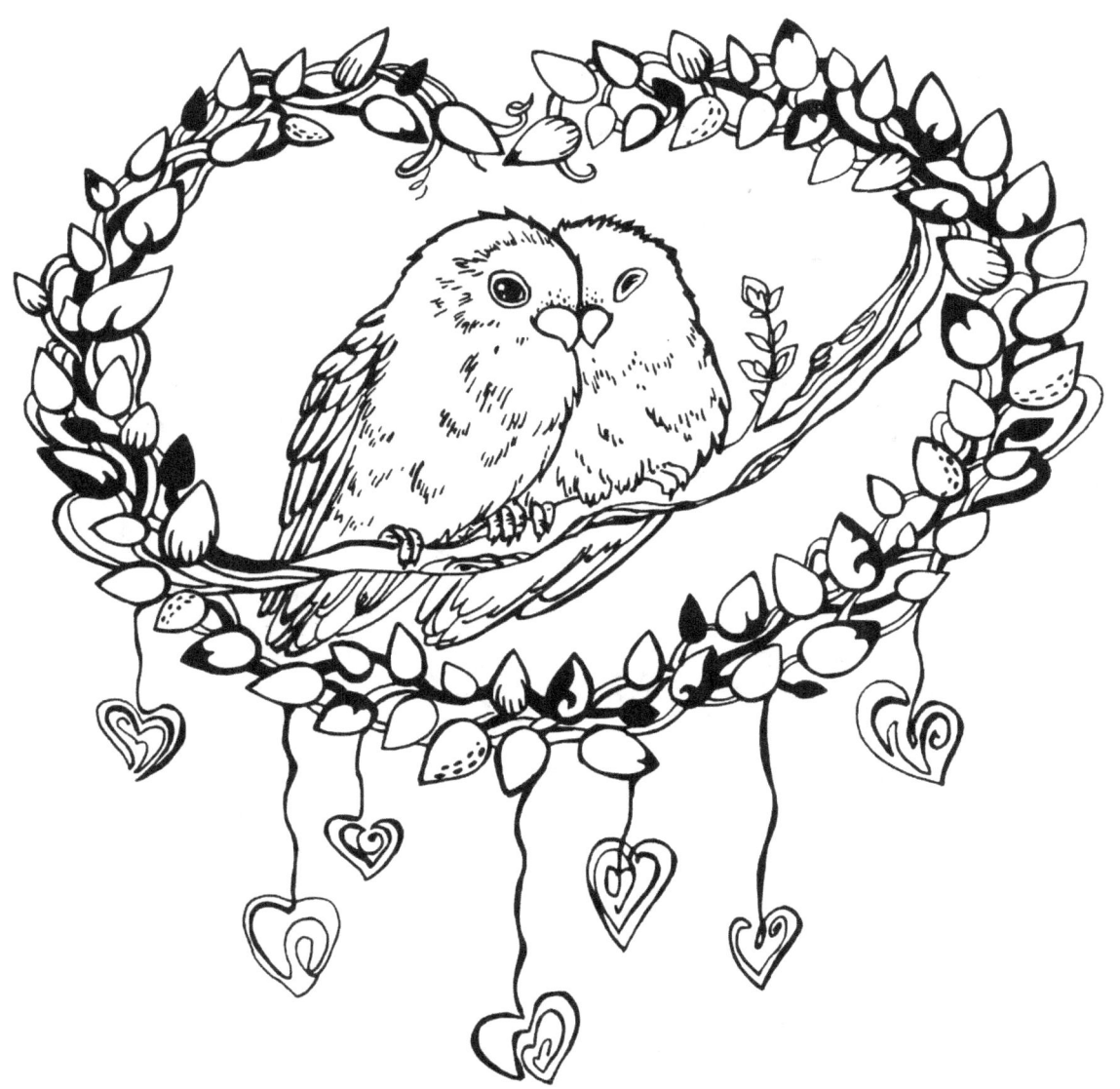

ONE IS LOVED BECAUSE ONE IS LOVED.

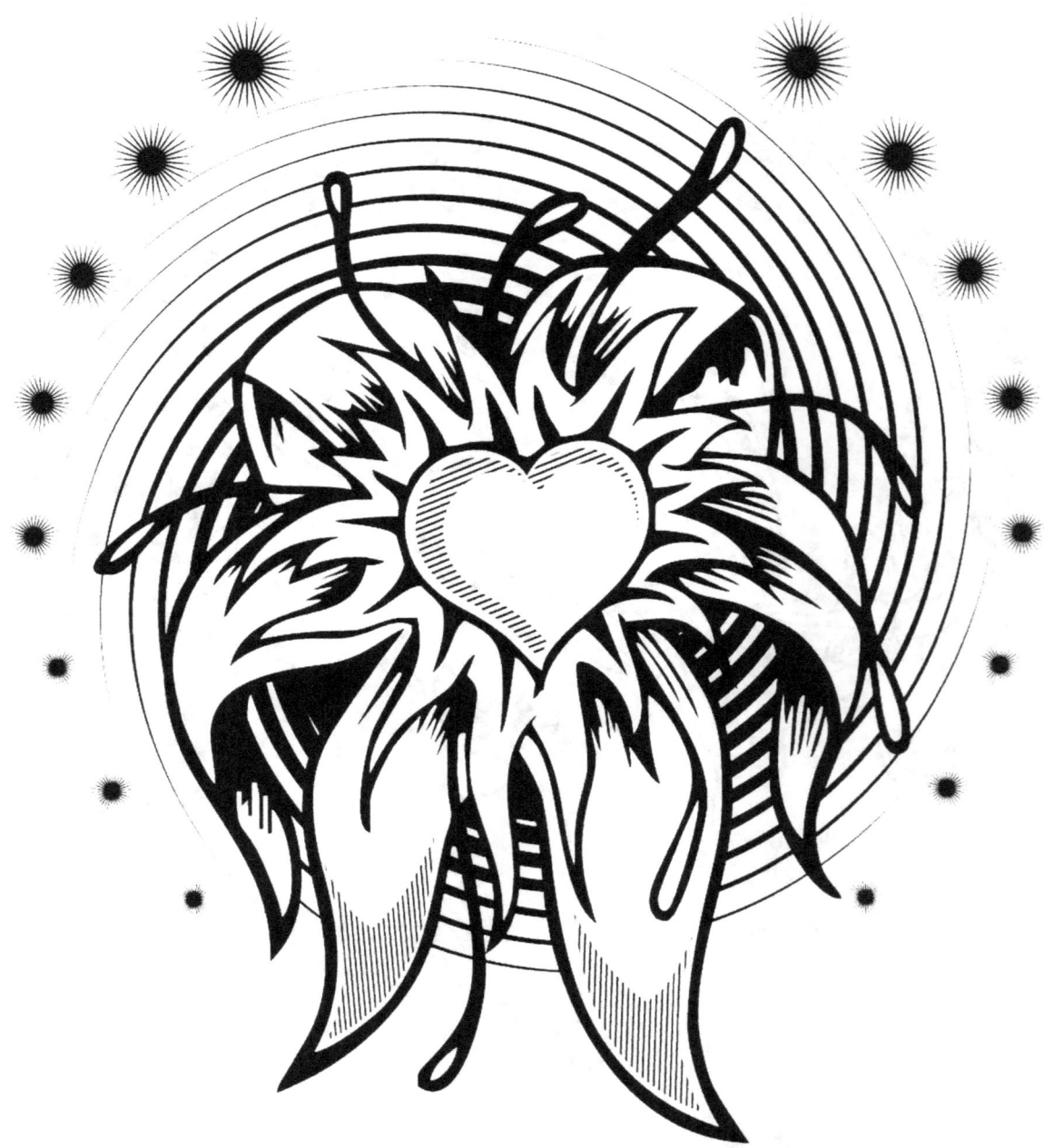

NO REASON IS NEEDED FOR LOVING.

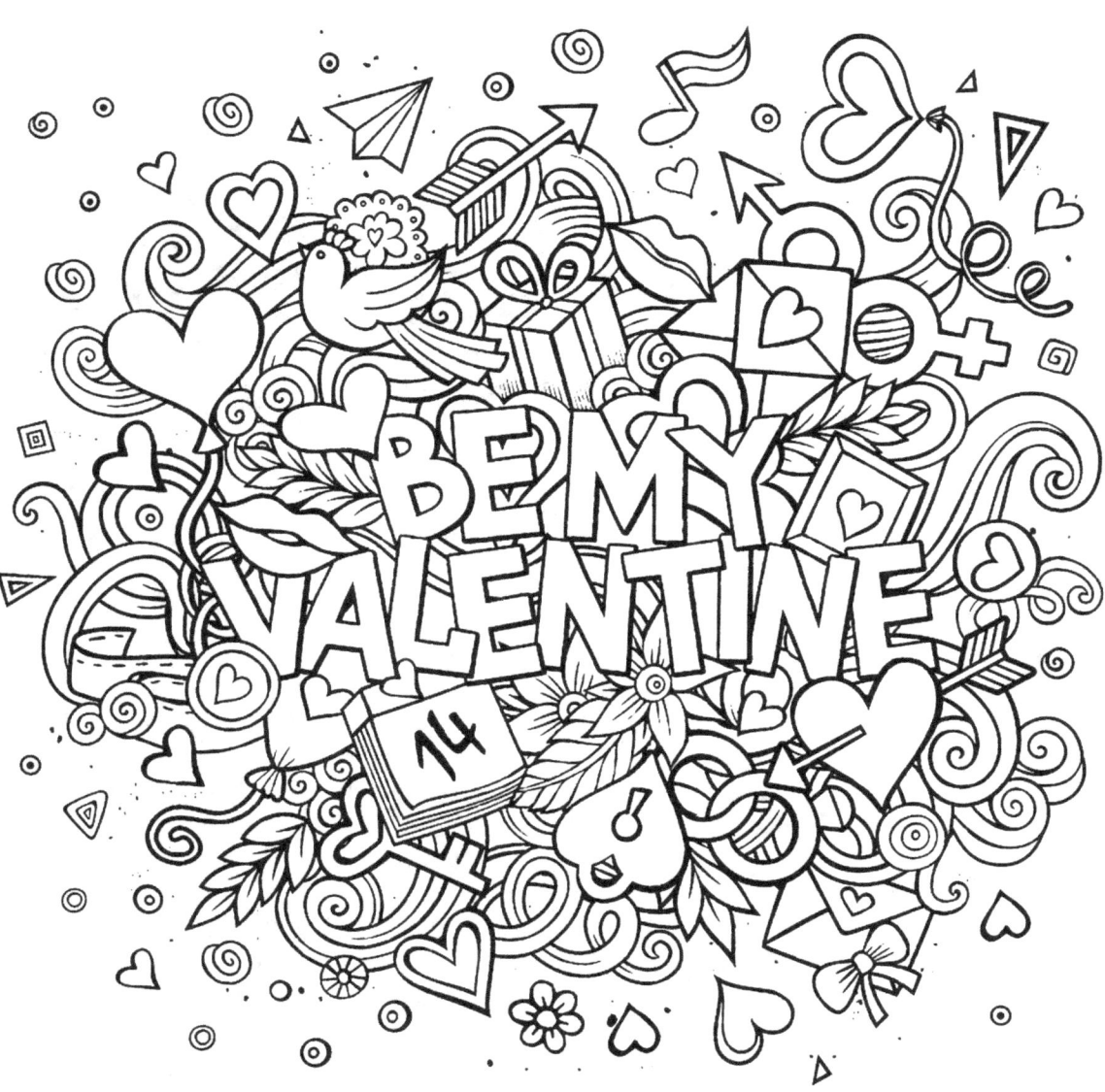

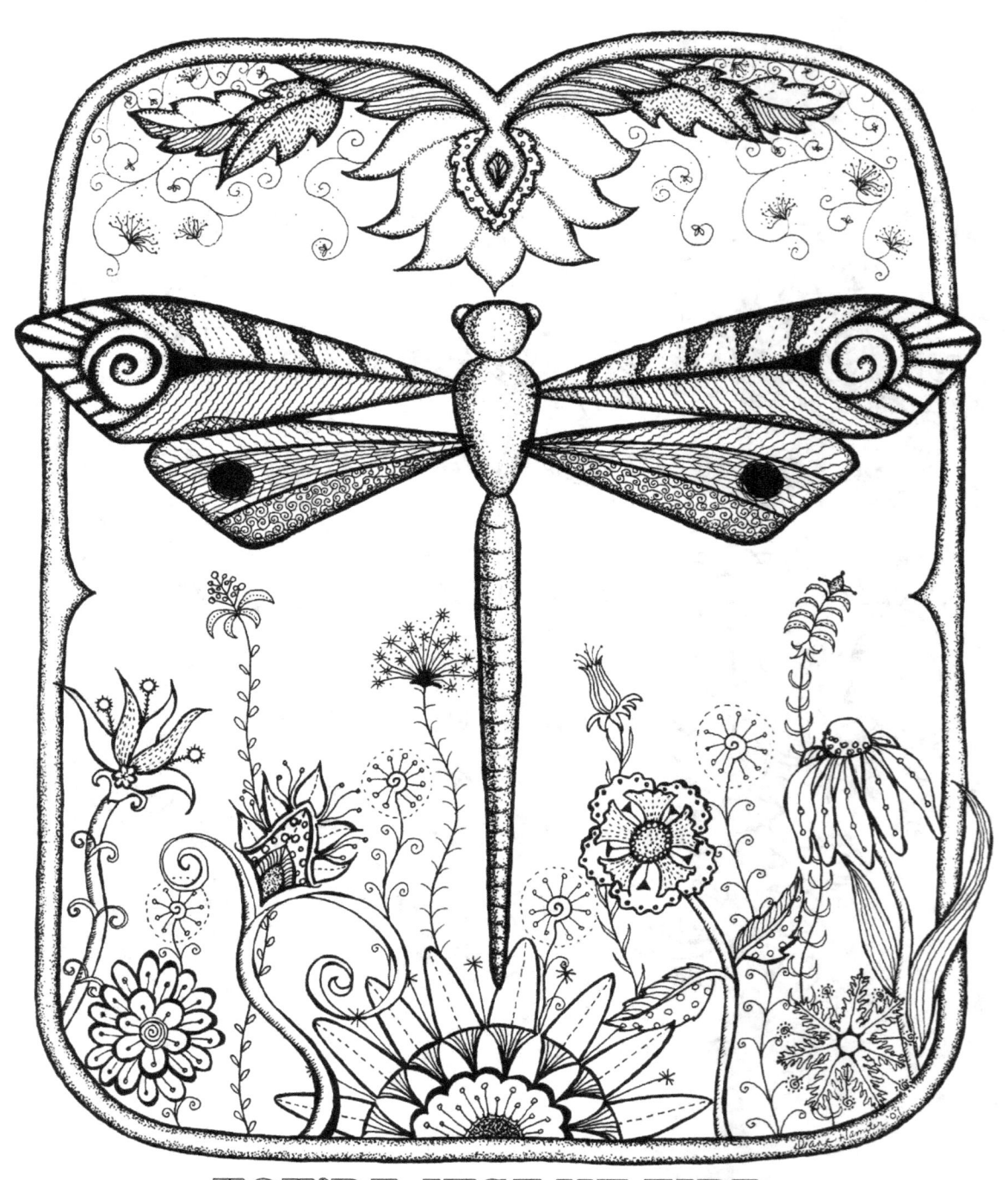

YOU'RE JUST MY TIPE.

TRUE LOVE BEGINS WHEN

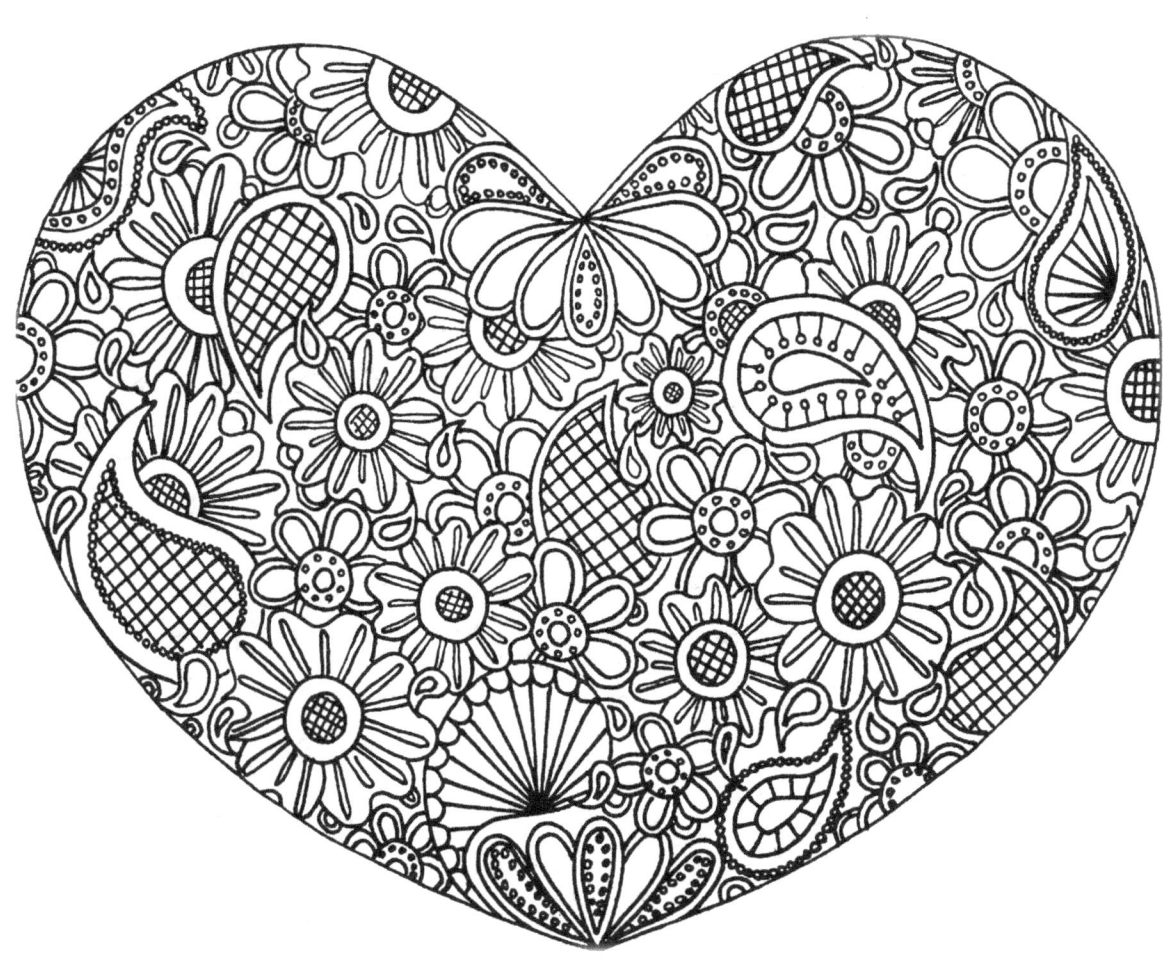

NOTHING IS LOOKED FOR IN RETIRN .

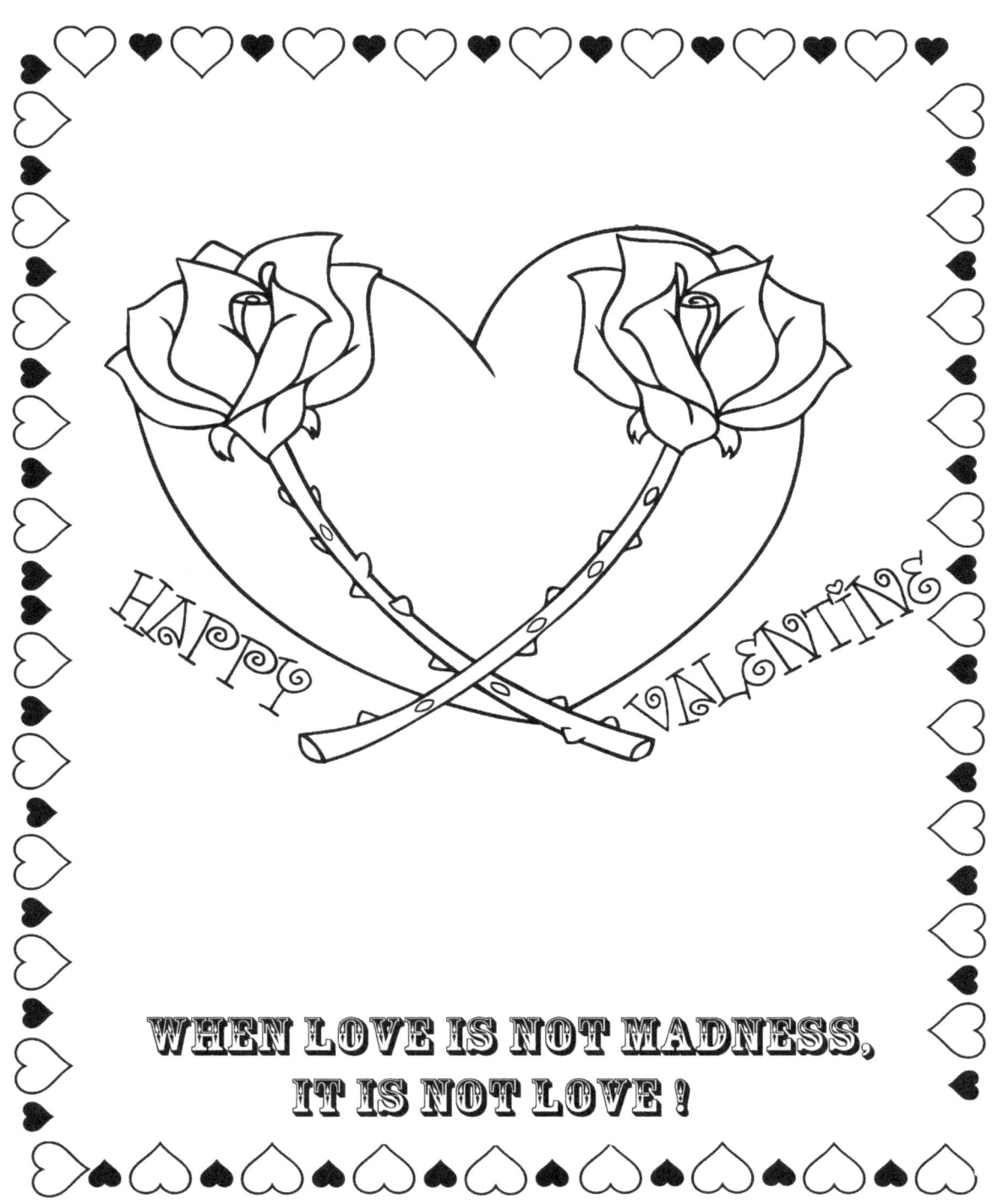

LOVE IS HAPPINESS

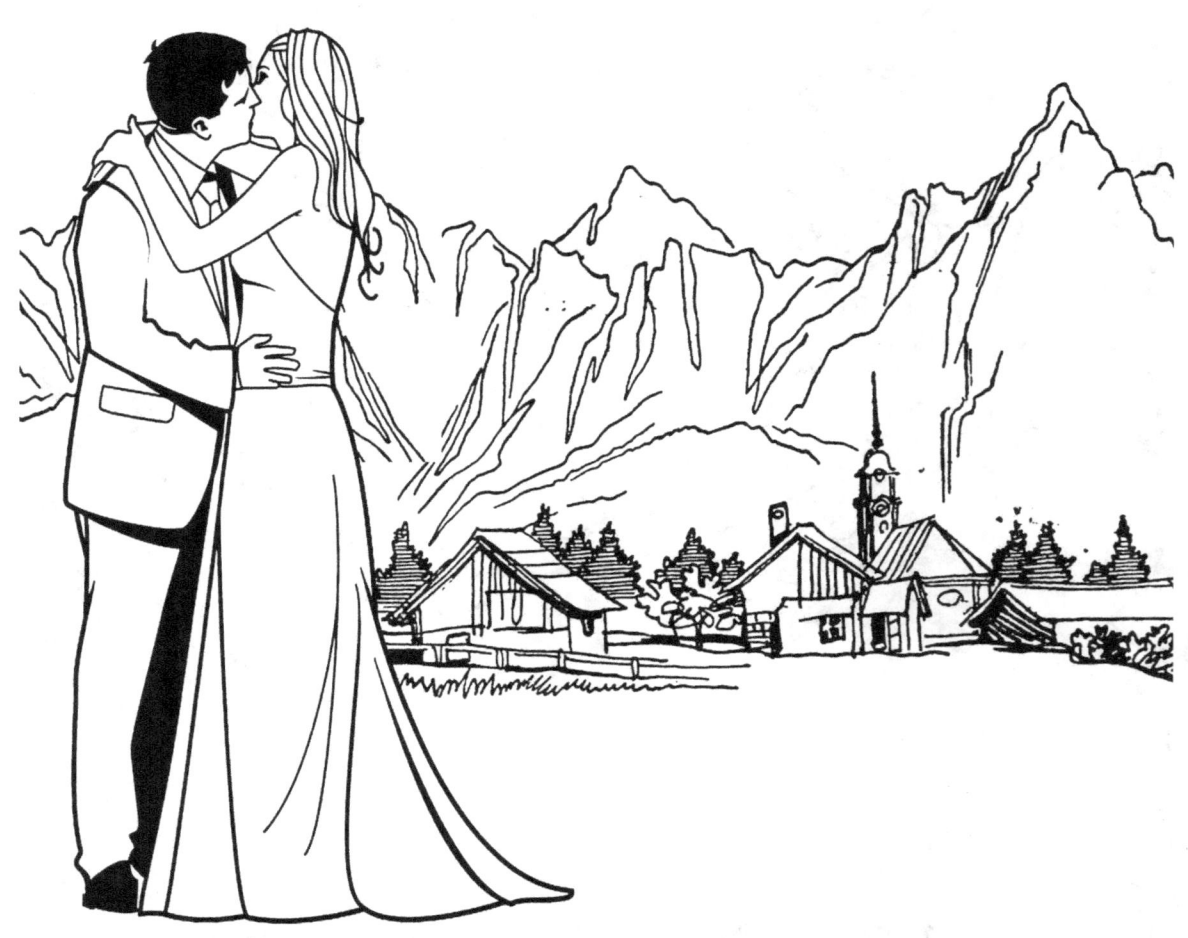

GIVEN BACK AND FORTH !

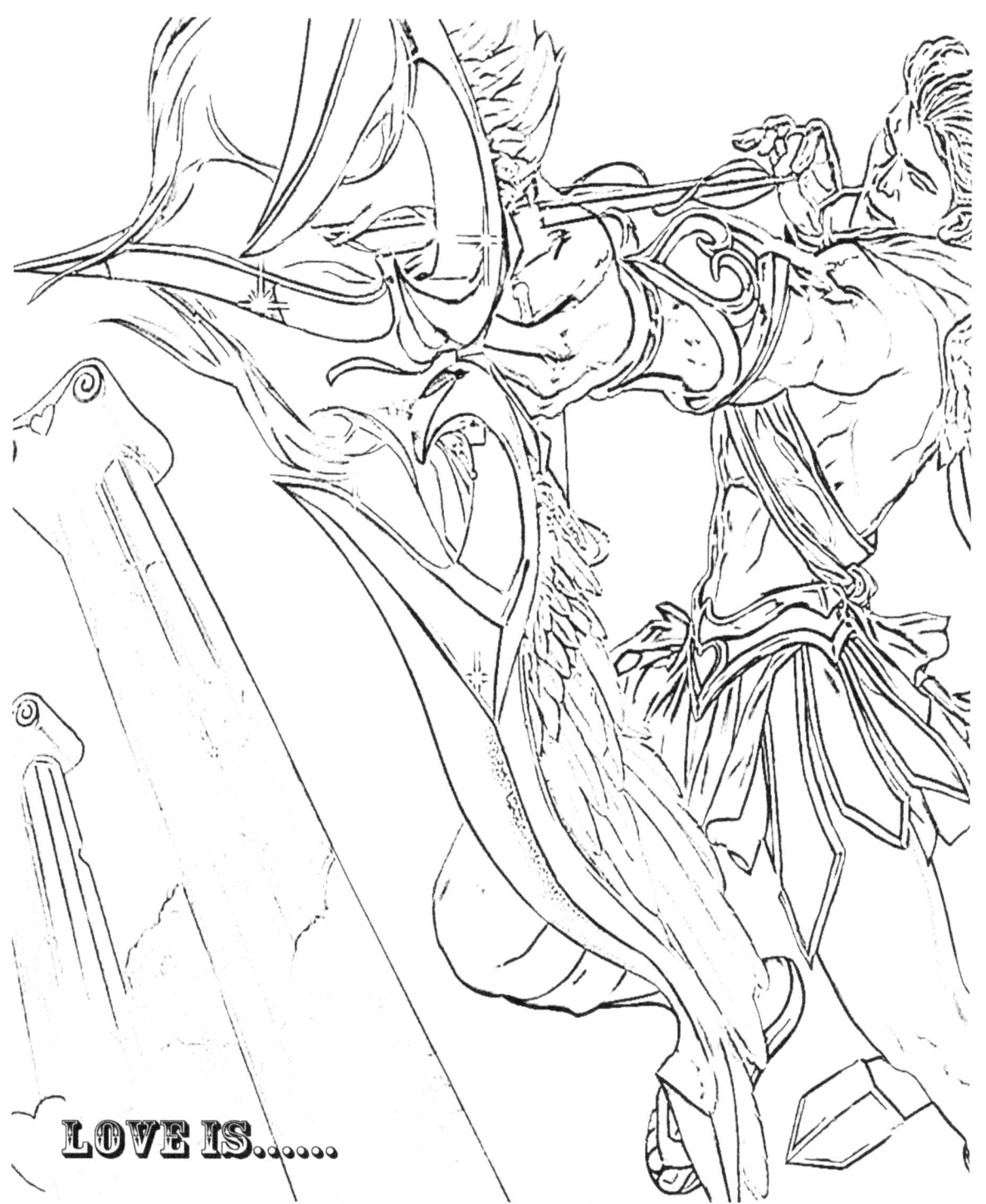

www.ingramcontent.com/pod-product-compliance
Lightning Source LLC
Chambersburg PA
CBHW081652220526
45468CB00009B/2622